108 SALES QUESTIONS

EVERY ENTREPRENEUR/SALES EXECUTIVE SHOULD ASK THEMSELVES

SUBRAMANIAN
CHANDRAMOULI

ISBN 979-8-89322-656-0

Table of Contents

Acknowledgements

Thanks to my wife, Vidya, who has patiently supported me in all my endeavours. Special thanks to my kids, Krishna Chandar and Aniruddh Ram.

I would like to thank my mentors, Srinivasan Ranganathan and Meena, founders of Inside-Out Foundation, for their continuous mentoring to me. Meeting them was the turning point in my life.

Special thanks to startup ecosystem partners T-Hub, Kerala Startup Mission, TiE Bangalore, German Accelerator (Start2 Group), European Union India Innocentre. They helped me to reach out to thousands of entrepreneurs across the world. This book is based on my interaction with thousands of those entrepreneurs.

Photography: Cynthia Sapna Photography

How This Book Will Be Useful?

This book talks about the questions an entrepreneur or a sales executive will have in his/her mind with respect to sales. These are **not** the sales questions you ask the customer. These are the questions you ask yourselves to get clarity. Getting answers to these questions will help you do your sales better.

I have also answered all the 108 sales questions. My answers are only my perspective. It may or may not be right. You should get answers for your context. More than answers, these questions are very important. I am hoping these questions will help you get more clarity and improve your sales. Best wishes.

LEADS – QUESTION-1

Lead Generation is a big challenge to me. How to generate leads consistently?

To generate leads consistently, you have to put effort consistently. First principle to understand is "lead generation is a way of life." For an entrepreneur or sales executive, everyday is a lead generation day, every prospect he/she meets is a possibility to generate leads. You can't take that thought out of your mind.

But of course, if you have a strong lead generation process, a system in place, and teams in place who are working on lead generation consistently, day in and day out, then you as an entrepreneur, can focus on other things. Still, you can't miss out on an opportunity to generate a lead when you are meeting with people.

LEADS – QUESTION-2

I am not good at networking? I am not comfortable talking to strangers. Can I still generate leads?

Even if you are not comfortable talking to strangers, you can choose other ways to generate leads. Like you can be a speaker or panel discussion member where you don't need to talk to strangers, they will come and talk to you. You can also generate leads using various digital marketing channels.

Say, for example, LinkedIn alone gives a lot of leads to some of the B2B companies I advise with. Many of the B2C companies I know use Instagram effectively to generate leads. Having said that, it is always better to work on your networking skills if you are an entrepreneur or sales executive. That skill will not only help you in lead generation but in many other ways.

LEADS – QUESTION-3

I am allocating a specific time in a week to generate leads. Is that a good strategy? How much time I should allocate for lead generation?

The answer is both yes and no. Yes, you can allocate specific time for lead generation activities like posting on LinkedIn, and Instagram, creating videos and posting on YouTube, etc. But I would call that as medium term or long-term lead generation activities. Those efforts in social media may give you leads immediately, or it may take some time.

To generate leads immediately, there is no specific time. When you are in an elevator, you can have a conversation with the person in the elevator, and maybe you can generate a lead. When you travel on a flight, train or bus, there is a huge possibility to generate leads. When you are at a conference, exhibition, or seminar, you have ample opportunities to generate leads.

To summarise, allocate specific time for lead generating activities, but be aware and ready to generate leads on any forthcoming opportunity

LEADS – QUESTION-4

I can't afford a big budget on marketing to generate leads. Do you have any specific tips for people like me to generate leads?

Of course you can generate leads without having any budget. My 3rd book, "Don't Spend Money for Generating Leads," talks about that. When you don't have money, obviously you must spend time and put in effort.If you are a B2B company, I strongly recommend spending more time on LinkedIn and continuously posting value-added content for your prospects. Increase your number of followers, be the first to discuss new processes or inventions in your area of expertise. Own a word, and the world should come to you for that word. Say, for example, you are very good at process innovation, any company in need of process improvements should come to you. You must consistently add value to your LinkedIn followers on your subject. If you are in B2C, do the same on Instagram or Facebook.

You can also attend many free conferences, exhibitions, and seminars to generate leads from it. When you make some money out of it, invest in attending paid conferences, exhibitions, and seminars. You may get better-quality leads.

LEADS – QUESTION-5

Is digital marketing the best way to generate leads?

In today's world, digital marketing is one of the most important ways to generate leads. If you are not leveraging digital marketing, then you are missing out on a good percentage of your prospects.

There are multiple ways to generate leads using digital marketing. Having a great website and generating traffic towards your website is one good way to generate leads. Today, LinkedIn, Instagram, Facebook, X, and YouTube are amazing ways to generate leads. Based on your business and target customers, you should decide which medium is best suited for you. Having said that, don't miss the opportunity to generate leads in the traditional way. Attend conferences, exhibitions, and seminars where your potential customers are present. Your friends, relatives, neighbours, and existing customers are all great sources to give you leads.

LEADS – QUESTION-6

How to generate quality leads? I don't want to spend time with low-quality leads.

U ntil you generate the lead, you don't know whether it is a high-quality lead or a lead that is wasting your time. The word "high-quality" can be assumed in 2 ways: firstly, the time taken to close the lead, and secondly, the amount of revenue it generates. In my view, any lead which is satisfying any of the above 2 criteria is a high-quality lead.

In order to filter out low-quality leads, you can choose the right audience. When you do marketing, your communication can be only to those prospects you are targeting. Say for example, if you prefer to work with companies who are having an annual revenue of USD 100 million plus, then you should talk about problems only companies with USD 100 million faces and how you can help them solve those problems. Seeing those marketing messages, only your relevant target audience will reach you.

When you go to a conference or exhibition, within the first 2-3 questions, you should qualify whether you are talking to a high-quality lead or not. My recommendation is to first generate leads, and then you can filter out the high-quality leads and spend more time only with them.

LEADS – QUESTION-7

I am not great at attending conferences and exhibitions. Is it mandatory to go to conferences?

In lead generation, nothing is mandatory. However, if you skip conferences, exhibitions, and seminars, you are missing out on a large portion of your prospective customers. If you have enough and above incoming leads from YouTube, LinkedIn, Instagram, or from your inside sales team, then you have the luxury to skip conferences, seminars, and exhibitions.

Even so, I would recommend that you should attend conferences and exhibitions because all top CEOs attend those events. It gives you the latest news, knowledge, and innovations happening in the industry, and also create possibilities to generate leads. Every time I attend a conference, I come out with new thoughts, big thinking, and high energy. Leads are a bonus. I would recommend starting with at least one conference in a quarter, and then you can increase it slowly. But do attend conferences and seminars.

LEADS – QUESTION-8

Leads should come to me directly without me putting any effort. What should I do so that I don't have to generate leads?

That's a good question. That would be the state that everyone would aspire to. If you are a solopreneur like a coach, trainer, auditor, or lawyer, and you are very well established in your field for many years and you don't want more business, then it is possible to achieve this state. But to reach there, you should have spent many, many years with high-quality output so that you will have more repeat customers and word-of-mouth marketing.

If you are a company or a business, then there is no way to avoid lead generation. Even great companies like Apple and Microsoft spend millions of dollars in marketing to generate leads. If you want more incoming leads, put more effort into social media like YouTube, Instagram, or LinkedIn. People will reach out to you automatically if you consistently give value to them through these social media platforms.

LEADS – QUESTION-9

Can I completely outsource my lead generation process so that I can spend more time on product and delivery?

Yes, you can outsource your lead generation process. But the agency or your lead generation partner should clearly understand who your target audience is and how to reach them. Completely outsourcing your lead generation activity is a risky proposition. Imagine if the agency you have outsourced suddenly decided to shut shop for some reason, then you must find another agency. For the second agency, understanding your business and then generating leads will take a few months. During that time, you will not have any leads.

The best thing is to do both. Have an in-house lead generation team and outsource lead generation activities. In this way, you are maximising your lead generation effort and also derisking any potential pitfalls.

PROSPECTING – QUESTION-10

How will I know that a lead is now a prospect?

Smart salespeople are very good at prospecting. They spend more time with the right prospects. When you get a lead, in your first interaction, you should find out whether they are the right prospect or not. Some of the key questions you should ask to find out whether:

1. They have a compelling need for your product or service
2. Do they have enough money to pay the price for your product or service
3. Are you talking to the right decision-maker or not
4. Will they buy in the immediate future or not
5. Will they be a great source of referral for you, and do they have the scope to give more business to you or not

Once you get answers to the above questions, you can determine whether that lead is a right prospect or not. In summary, only by asking the right questions will you be able to evaluate whether a lead is a prospect or not.

PROSPECTING – QUESTION-11

What is the difference between a lead and a prospect? And why is it important to understand this difference?

A lead suggests there is a possibility that they may need your product or service. At the lead stage, you are unsure whether there is a compelling need for your service, or if they will buy it in the immediate future. You are also uncertain whether you are talking to the decision-maker or not. There may be many decision-makers.

When the lead is qualified into a prospect, you are certain that they need your product or service. You don't know whether they will buy it from you, but you know that they need your product or service.

You are also clear that they will buy in the near future. You are also aware of the key decision-makers. All this knowledge comes to you as you ask the right questions during your lead qualifying stage. A prospect is nothing but a qualified lead.

PROSPECTING – QUESTION-12

Can I convert every lead into a prospect?

Not every lead can be a prospect. And not every lead should be a prospect as well. Prospecting is a lead qualifying process. All leads may not have a compelling reason to buy your product or service. Some of them may not be able to afford your price. Some of them may not buy in the near future. Some of them may have cash flow risk.

So, it is important to qualify the lead. Many entrepreneurs and sales executives get into the trap of working with the wrong leads and struggle to collect their payment. Once the project is on, they cannot come out of it. Hence prospecting is an important aspect of sales. Smart salespeople spend a lot of time with the right prospects to ensure they are working with the right people. They will quickly stop talking to wrong leads to save time which can be spent with the right prospects.

PROSPECTING – QUESTION-13

Once I understand that a certain lead is a prospect, what should be my right next steps?

Once you are convinced that you are talking to the right prospect, the next step is to have a meeting, which can be face-to-face or online. If you have a product demo, then you go for a demo. Before the meeting or demo, you should prepare a lot. Do research about the company, the key people, the latest news articles, their customers, their product launch, etc.

Preparation is key before the meeting. The objective of the meeting is to get the customer to approve you to send a proposal to them. In this meeting as well, asking questions is the most important thing. Deals are closed not by answers, deals are closed by questions. Your ability to ask the right, relevant, transformational questions gives you an edge among the competitors.

QUESTIONING SKILLS – QUESTION-14

What questions should I ask a customer?

What questions you should ask a customer depends on the nature of your business and the industry of the customer. Having said that, there is a basic framework you can implement. Don't ask questions for which answers can be easily obtained by doing simple research.

Also, don't directly jump into asking questions. Have a business conversation, talk about general things. Then start with questions that are easy and comfortable for a prospect to answer. Then you can go to deeper questions about the prospect's potential problem and what they are currently doing to address it. Your intention is to help the customers. In order to help the customer, you have to understand the customer, their business, and their problems. And your questions should be transformational rather than transactional. Remember, deals are won by questions, not by answers.

QUESTIONING SKILLS – QUESTION-15

If I ask more questions will the customer get irritated?

No. The customer will not get irritated if you ask more questions. He/she will get irritated only if you ask it in an irritating way. When you position yourself as a knowledge partner, showing them something new, teaching them something new, discussing with them something new which is useful to them, you get their respect. Then when you ask questions, they will be happy to answer you. Now, they see you as a person who is there to help them.

Many salespeople directly jump into questioning without establishing the credibility of being a knowledge partner. Obviously, customers don't want to answer questions to everybody. To summarise, you must earn the respect to ask questions. Your initial questions should be deep, transformational questions which nobody has asked them till now. Once you get that respect, you can ask more questions. Customers will not get irritated.

❖ ❖ ❖

QUESTIONING SKILLS – QUESTION-16

Before I ask any questions, the customer is asking me a lot of questions. I am not getting a chance to ask any questions. How to overcome this?

Yes. In a normal scenario, customers will ask a lot of questions when they meet their supplier. Because they are in an evaluating scenario, whether you can add value to them or not. If you just keep answering them, then you are one among the many vendors who are being evaluated. To position yourself as a knowledge partner you must ask questions.

But when the customer is not giving you any chance in the conversation how to ask questions, the best way to do that is to answer your customer's question and end your answer with a question. The beauty of a question is whenever it is asked, the other person will answer it. Now the customer being intelligent he/she will answer your question, then she will end her answer with a question. You will also do the same, end your answer with a question and the conversation continues.

QUESTIONING SKILLS – QUESTION-17

I have a fear that if I ask more questions, I will lose the deal. How should I overcome this?

The default job of our mind is to create fear within ourselves. Actually, most of the fear is an illusion. You will never lose a deal by asking the right question. In reality, it's the opposite, deals are closed by great questions, not great answers.

Imagine this, are you the only vendor who can answer all the questions of your customer? No, most of your competitors can also answer all these questions. But only very few, in my experience only 2% of the people in this world are able to ask the right, relevant, transformational questions. Those 2% of people don't have any competition at all. To summarise, you will never lose a deal by asking the right questions, rather you will position yourself as a knowledge partner by asking the right questions, thereby increasing your probability to close the deal.

QUESTIONING SKILLS – QUESTION-18

To understand the customer's pain point I should ask questions. Is there any other importance/ leverage in asking questions?

Understanding customer's pain points is one important aspect of winning a deal and asking questions is key to achieve that. But asking questions has many more advantages. By asking the right, transformational questions, you position yourself as a knowledge partner to your customer. That positioning happens in the first meeting itself. Though the deal is closed on 5th or 7th meeting, the rest of the meetings are only the reiteration of the decision the customer has taken in his/her first meeting with you.

By asking those right questions, you are communicating that you are keen to help your customer. You are keen to understand the business of the customer. It also implies that you have worked with many great businesspeople and hence you are able to ask those questions. Smart customers will understand this. They evaluate you by the quality of your questions not by the quality of your answers. Though your answers are important to them, they will not be surprised by it.

QUESTIONING SKILLS – QUESTION-19

How to ask transformational questions rather than transactional questions?

It is very important to ask transformational questions rather than transactional questions. I have created a 3-point formula to achieve this:

1. Annual Report:

    If the company is a listed entity, read through the annual report fully. Give more focus to the message of the Chairman/CEO in the first few pages. Read their vision for the next 3-5-10 years. Generate a few questions based on it. If the company is not listed, go through the website of the company, their news section, the company's last 1-year LinkedIn post, the CEO's last 1-year LinkedIn post, and the person you are going to meet, his/her last one-year LinkedIn post. You can generate great questions from this data.

2. Customer's Customer:

    From the website, note down the customer's customer. Read about the customer's customer. Find out their big wins, big problems, important news. From this, understand how it will impact your customer. Generate questions based on it.

3. New Innovation/ New framework / New Technology /New Compliance – research about all of these in the customer's industry. Create a few relevant questions out of this.

    All the above 3 points will help you generate 15-20 transformational questions, and this will be a game-changer. It will be a competitive strategy.

QUESTIONING SKILLS – QUESTION-20

What if the customer says I am not interested in answering your questions?

enerally, the customer will not say like that explicitly. But they may show displeasure with you, communicating that they are not comfortable. That's why it is very important to observe the body language/ tone of the customer.

It means that we are not asking the right questions to the customer. Our first job is to gain respect from the customer by asking transformational questions. Once we get that respect, then we can ask more questions. How will we know that we have gained that respect? You can easily observe that the customer's body language is changing, tone changing. You can feel that respect from him/her. If they explicitly say they are not interested in answering your questions, apologise and schedule another meeting. That day, do your best to gain respect.

QUESTIONING SKILLS – QUESTION-21

In a sales conversation, approximately how many questions can I ask?

It's not about the number of questions you ask, it's more about the percentage of time you are making the customer talk. If you ask more questions, then you are making the customer talk more. But customers will get irritated if you ask irrelevant questions. That's why it is important to ask the right, relevant, transformational questions.

In a typical sales conversation, I recommend you should talk less than 30% of the time and the customer should talk more than 70% of the time. Then you are in great probability to position yourself as a knowledge partner. Even in a worst-case scenario, you should not talk more than 50%. This percentage is applicable only if the customer is not allowing you to ask more questions. Remember, in a sales conversation, whoever asking the question is the King. It doesn't matter whether it is the customer or the supplier.

QUESTIONING SKILLS – QUESTION-22

I have a fear that I may not be able to ask quality questions. It is safer to just answer the customer's questions. Why should I risk showing my intellectual gap?

Yes. If you ask stupid questions, then you are sure to lose the deal. But by not asking any questions, you are not able to understand the customer's problem. Even if you ask a few questions on the customer's problem and give a proposal based on it, you still don't have any winning edge. Your competitor would also have done the same thing.

First, you must increase your self-belief that you have the ability to ask the right, relevant, transformational questions. To increase your self-belief, you have to prepare well, do the homework, do the right research and talk to relevant people. Nothing can beat your homework. Being safe and not asking any questions and failing is far worse than preparing well, asking questions, and failing. You may fail in the first few deals, but after that, you would have gained enough knowledge and start winning.

❖ ❖ ❖

QUESTIONING SKILLS – QUESTION-23

Will questioning my customers give me any competitive advantage?

Yes. Asking the right, relevant, transformational questions will provide a significant competitive advantage. Actually, it is a competitive strategy. Because 98% of people won't prepare well to ask these deep questions. We have discussed the 3-point formula to ask transformational questions. It takes time, discipline, and effort to follow the 3-point formula. Most of your competition will not do it.

It is easy to just answer the questions asked by the customer. You can even prepare well to answer them to the best. Most people do that. But it is very hard to ask the right, relevant transformational questions to the customer. It needs not only preparation but also courage. Hence, few people can do that. Deals are closed not by answers but by questions.

❖ ❖ ❖

FOLLOW UP – QUESTION-24

How many times should I follow up to get a
meeting?

The direct answer to this question is "Until you get the meeting." If you think deeply, why is the prospect not giving you the time to meet? Maybe because he/she feels that you are trying to sell to them.

To get a meeting, we must earn respect and/or create curiosity. When you call or message them, present some data where the prospect is curious to meet you. For example, "Hi, I am Eashwar, calling from Mahadev Enterprise, and we recently helped a company like yours save 30% of their IT costs in just 3 months. Would you be interested in meeting us over Zoom for just 15 minutes?" – This may create some curiosity, and he/she may give you time for a meeting.

FOLLOW UP – QUESTION-25

What should I do when a customer says, "Don't Follow up?"

et's understand why the customer is saying "Don't follow up." He/She got irritated because we are continuously asking for something from them. Asking for a meeting, asking for business, etc. Think for a minute, can you give them something instead of asking them? Give something legally and ethically? Can you really add value to a prospect? We can add value to a customer. But when you add value to a prospect, they become your customers.

So, if a customer says, "Don't follow up," think and add value to them by giving some useful insights about their industry/business, which will help them grow. Nothing about your company or product or service, only about the customer, and what you are giving should add value to them. Then, even without a follow up, you will get the meeting or business. They want to meet you. They want to do business with you.

FOLLOW UP – QUESTION-26

Some of my customers are not paying for my
product/service despite following up.
What should I do?

Payment follow up is an important follow up. There is no running away from it. Some key points in payment follow up are:

1. Ask the right person who can give it to you.

    Sometimes you will be following up with the delivery head with whom you have interacted during the project phase. And you are following up with him, in turn, he must follow up with the CFO, and it takes time. Rather than this, get connected to the CFO yourself. Build a relationship with the CFO and start directly following up with him. This way, you have direct communication with the decision-maker, and you will know the real reason why you are not getting the money and when you will get the money.

2. Ask again and again. Following up once or twice is not enough. You must ask again and again. Saying No to the same person multiple times is tough. Leverage this psychology. Ask politely, again and again, until you get your payment.

FOLLOW UP – QUESTION-27

After how many follow-ups will customers get irritated? When should I stop my follow up?

The customer getting irritated is not dependent on the number of follow-ups; it depends on how you are following up. As we discussed in earlier questions, when you add value to a prospect, he/she will not get irritated. The second thing is, that you should not stop following up if you really believe that you can add value to your customer and help him/her in their business.

I have so many personal examples where I have won deals after the 36th follow up, 28th follow up, etc. Follow up is not just sending a mail or a WhatsApp message. Follow up has 2 definitions: **adding value and being in the mind.** If you can add value and be in their mind, then you are following up. Keep doing these 2 things consistently. You will get what you want from your client.

FOLLOW UP – QUESTION-28

What is the best mode to follow up? Call, mail, meeting in person, WhatsApp? What do you suggest?

It all depends on the customer. Smart salespeople in their first meeting ask the customer what is the best mode to reach them? Phone/Mail/WhatsApp, etc. Based on the customer's preference, you should communicate with him/her.

I met a prospective customer 3 years back and when I asked her what is the best mode to reach her? She said, Telegram. I downloaded the Telegram app only for her and started interacting with her. She replies to me almost immediately. That's what she prefers. I can't say I don't have the Telegram app. Salespeople should be flexible enough to accommodate customer preferences. Follow up as per your customer's convenient mode.

FOLLOW UP – QUESTION-29

I feel bad when my follow up gets rejected. I am asking my junior staff to follow up. Is that a good strategy?

Your junior staff can do a follow up. But the question is with whom he/she is following up. If he is following up with the CEO of your prospective company, then the CEO may not like it. If you want to interact with senior management, then I recommend you should follow up yourself.

You should not feel bad about your follow up rejection. Follow up is the number #1 skill of great salespeople. They never take the rejection personally. If you want to win the fortune, then you must master the skill of follow up. For that, you must be emotionally strong and have the maturity that a follow up rejection is nothing personal.

CUSTOMER RELATIONSHIP – QUESTION-30

How to build a long-term relationship with customers?

Relationship building with customers takes time. Most relationships are based on trust. To build trust, first you must make the customer comfortable. If you continuously make somebody comfortable many times, rapport is built. Once rapport is built over a period, trust is built. Trust is maintained by your repeated continuous, trustworthy actions and behaviour.

To keep it simple, do what you say and say what you can do. Give more importance to your commitment and have an excellent work ethic. Everybody will love to have a long relationship with you. Every customer prefers to work with the person they know for a longer period. This itself can create an entry barrier to any of your competitors.

CUSTOMER RELATIONSHIP – QUESTION-31

How to get repeat orders from my existing customers?

Any customer when she is happy with her current supplier will give more orders to him. Sometimes as an entrepreneur/salesperson, you should guide the customer for growth. You can help her with more insights about the market and show her how she can grow with this new project idea. By helping her grow, you automatically get more orders from her.

Expecting repeat orders for the same business is ordinary; creating new opportunities for yourself by helping your customer to expand is the most preferred way to get repeat orders. This ability to identify new opportunities for your customer will be loved by all your customers. This will put you in a different position in the mind of the customer. You are not considered as a vendor; you are considered as a consultant who is there to help her.

CUSTOMER RELATIONSHIP – QUESTION-32

With some customers, I can maintain a good relationship, but with some other customers, my relationship is not deep. Why is that?

There are 6 different personality types of customers. By default, you are also one among those personality types. When your personality type matches with the personality type of the customer, you both are aligned, your communication is in sync with the customer, and it has become easy for both of you to work together and the relationship is strong.

That's why smart salespeople first understand the personality type of the customer and mirror that personality type to get aligned with the customer. This will help the salesperson to think like the customer and then act accordingly. To build a stronger relationship with all your customers, understand their personality type and be flexible to that personality type so that you can match their thinking.

CUSTOMER RELATIONSHIP – QUESTION-33

What is the frequency I should visit my existing customers?

I recommend that each salesperson/entrepreneur should first classify their customers. Like Top 25, Top 10, Top 50, etc., based on their total number of customers, revenue, region, product, etc. For example, as a CEO, you should personally visit your top 10 customers every quarter. If you are a sales executive, the top 10 customers in your portfolio should be visited every quarter. The top 25 customers should be visited at least once a year. The remaining customers you should have a call with at least once a quarter.

Why is this important? This is important for you to receive feedback, to understand the market, to cross-sell, up-sell, to sustain your revenue with the customer, to get more business from the same customer, to get referrals. So many good things happen when you visit the customer periodically.

CUSTOMER RELATIONSHIP – QUESTION-34

How will I know that I am having a deeper relationship with my customers?

Say, for example, you have 60+ customers in your business. Out of this, there are 5 customers who are calling you and asking for your opinion which is out of your business scope.

Say you are selling software services, but your customer is asking you whether they can open a new manufacturing plant in a particular part of the city? They are taking your opinion and asking for a reference for a good architect. Not only this, for many of their business/personal problems, they are seeking your guidance. It's the same case with the remaining 4 customers.

Then it means with these 5 customers, you have a deeper relationship. They will be your long-term customers as long you sustain the trust they have in you. Now it is your responsibility to maintain and grow this trust. These are the customers who are going to refer you to many other potential customers.

CUSTOMER RELATIONSHIP – QUESTION-35

My existing customers are not giving me any referrals. How to get new referrals from my existing customers?

The answer is in 2 parts. First, you have to understand why the existing customers are not giving you any referrals. Is it because they are not satisfied with your product/service? Or any other reason? How to know that? Politely ask for feedback. Set up a meeting, only to get feedback. Don't defend any of their points. Just listen. Note it down. Say Thanks and come back to your office and reflect on it.

The second part is, have you ever asked your customer for a referral? Nobody in this world has time to think about others. Leverage the power of asking. Once in 3 months or 6 months, meet your customer and ask for a specific referral. There is a high chance most of them will connect you to their contacts.

CUSTOMER RELATIONSHIP – QUESTION-36

With some of my big corporate customers, when the person I work with quits their job, I also lose my contract. The new joiner prefers to give the contract to his known contacts. How to overcome this?

This is common in the industry. People like to work with people whom they know, whom they have experienced. I see this as an opportunity for you. The person who has left and who knows you would have joined some other organisation. Stay in touch with him/her. Most probably he/she is going to give you business there as well.

In your current customer company, a new person has joined, and they don't know you. Meet them and show your past credentials. Offer them to conduct some sample sessions/demos/physical samples (based on your product) where they can experience your work and from there build trust. There is a possibility they will consider you for future needs. You can also take testimonials or positively influence through the senior leaders in that organisation who have used your product/service.

❖ ❖ ❖

CUSTOMER RELATIONSHIP – QUESTION-37

How to become the most preferred vendor/partner for my existing customers?

People will like us when we go beyond what is expected. Let me give you an example. I have a friend who is a tours and travels operator. I recommended him to one of my family friends who booked through my travel friend for a holiday in Sri Lanka.

Two days before the holiday, the airline cancelled the flight for some reason. The travel operator immediately booked an alternate flight from a different location and arranged travel for my family friend to that location, booked hotels for them in that new location, and from there, they flew to Sri Lanka. Their itinerary had no change with respect to their holidays in Sri Lanka.

They are super happy, and now my family friend is referring this tour operator to so many of his contacts. The tour operator has become their preferred vendor/partner. You will become a preferred vendor when you do things which other vendors will not do. Those actions bring customer delight.

PRICING – QUESTION-38

How to arrive at competitive pricing?

I always recommend people to remove the word competition from their minds. Research the market price, understand the market price, and then decide your price based on your context. If you are just starting a business, pricing a little lower than the market is okay because you are learning the business. Once you have enough experience in the market and you are consistently working on adding value to your product/service, don't be afraid to increase your price.

Your prospective customers may negotiate and say they are getting it cheaper in the market; don't worry, stick to your price. If you add enough value with quality, there will be enough customers for your product or service. If the entire world should charge the same price for the same products/services, then there won't be different brands at all. Every brand targets a different set of target segments based on the customer's ability to buy at that price and also based on the brand's ability to serve those target customers.

PRICING – QUESTION-39

How to create a premium-priced product or service?

You can create a premium-priced product or service in any business. In every industry, there are the top 5% of customers who prefer to buy only a premium brand. The formula to create a premium product or service is "Have a functional product or service, invest some time, money, effort, creative thinking and add value to it, and sell it at a premium" – please read the above line at least 3 times. Let me give you an example.

You are travelling to Dubai from Bangalore on Emirates airlines. A normal ticket to Dubai costs you around INR 15,000 (USD 180-200) in a non-peak period. On the same flight, a Business class ticket costs you INR 1,50,000 (USD 1800-2000), 10x the price. Same flight, same destination, same pilot. The functional service of Emirates Airlines is taking you to Dubai. In business class, they add value to you by giving extra leg space, better seats, better entertainment gadgets, better food, better wine, and extra baggage which may be worth another 15,000 (USD 180-200), but they are charging you 10X. According to me, that is the right thing to do in pricing. Cinema theatres, Automobiles, Smartphones, Real Estate, across the industries you can see this formula working. With little thinking and effort, you can also do the same.

PRICING – QUESTION-40

What should I do if customers don't agree with my price?

You can negotiate until your walk-away price. If customers are not agreeing to your walk-away price, then you should walk away. If the customers are not agreeing to your price, then they are not your target customers.

Look back, reflect, and analyse what kind of customer he/she is? Is she part of your target customer segment? Can she afford your price? If she cannot afford your price, then she is not your customer. That's why it is very important to have clarity on your target segment.

Say for example, after your analysis, you can see a pattern that customers whose revenue is less than INR 50 crores cannot afford your product, and you are getting more customers whose revenue is INR 100 crores and above, then you should either serve only INR 100 crores customers or have different products for INR 50 crores and INR 100 crores customers.

PRICING – QUESTION-41

What should I do if my competitors reduce their prices drastically?

Don't worry about your competition reducing prices. If you are in a trading business, then revisit your pricing strategy. If you create your own product or service, then don't worry about competitors' pricing. Pricing is all about the ability of the customer to pay and the perceived value of the customer about your product or service.

What you focus on expands. If you focus on competitors, then fear expands. So, focus on how you can add more value to your prospective customers and work with the right target segment; you will get your price. Communicate the benefits your customers are getting for the price they are paying. With great customer service, customers will be happy to pay the price you demand.

PRICING – QUESTION-42

I don't know what price customers are willing to pay for my product or service. How to arrive at pricing?

Imagine you have created a new product or service, and you don't know how to price it. In that case, the first thing is to identify the target customers for whom this product or service will be of great value. Once you have identified that, talk to them, and ask them how much they are willing to pay for this service. Talk to at least 10 customers and get their pricing numbers. Remove the outliers.

For example, you have built a consumable product and out of 10 customers, 7 are ready to pay around INR 1000 for that and 1 is ready to pay INR 2000 and 2 are ready to pay around INR 500. Then remove 2000 and 500 from the list and arrive at INR 1000 as your price. See whether you can make a reasonable profit with a price of INR 1000; if yes, then launch it at that price. Sell it to the first 100 customers at that price, and with that feedback and data points, increase or decrease the price accordingly.

PRICING – QUESTION-43

What are the various methods in which I can increase my price?

You can increase your price in 3 ways. Firstly, change the people. When I say people, it means customers. If your current set of prospects is not able to pay the price for your product or service, change the customer segment which can afford your price. The new customer segment may have different needs, and different priorities, fulfil that and they can pay your price.

Secondly, change your location. If you are selling in a semi-urban area and not able to get the price, then go to an urban area. Sometimes it is better to change the country where you are selling. When you enter a new territory, tweak your product/service according to that city/country and find the right target segment in that country then you will get your price.

Thirdly, have unique situations where you can sell at a premium price. Like Business class tickets, Premium seating in a cinema hall, express laundry service, and express check-in at airports are examples. If you notice, they add value by saving time or giving you a great experience and they charge a premium for that.

PRICING – QUESTION-44

When will I know that I must increase my price?

A good question. First, you should have the mindset that you have to increase your price. Because increasing your price also means increasing the value you are giving to your customers. Once you are ready with this mindset then it is about the proposal in B2B (Business to Business) or communicating the new price in B2C (Business to Consumer).

When you are continuously winning proposals with your current price in a B2B scenario, then it is time to change your price. Once you increase your price, you will start losing. Your prospective customer will not be convinced of your justification for your new price, then you will learn. You will move to the right target customers, you will also modify your pitch based on your learning. Then one day, your new price will be accepted by a customer. Then that price will become your default price. When you are increasing your price, be ready to lose the first 5-10 proposals.

PRICING – QUESTION-45

I have a fear that if I increase my price, my current customers will go away from me. How to overcome this fear?

You can address this in 2 ways. First, hold the existing price for current customers. Increase the price only for new customers. This is the gift you are giving to your existing customers for their loyalty to you. At least you can hold the price for one or 2 years.

Second, if you still want to increase the price for all existing customers, communicate to them politely over email and phone the reasons why you are increasing the price. Tell them how you are adding more value even with the new price. Give them enough time on when this new price will kick in. For example, if you want to increase the price from January 1st of the year, then your communication should go at least 90 days before that.

There is a good chance you may lose some customers because of this price rise; don't worry about that. you can always win new customers.

PRICING – QUESTION-46

When should I give a discount and to which customers should I give a discount?

The important question to ask is: do you have to give a discount? If you have decided that you want to give a discount, then be clear on why you want to give a discount. If you are entering a new country/region/industry, then to get market share you can give a discount. If you are entering a new target segment, to understand that segment you can give a discount. There should be a compelling reason on why you are giving a discount. Why part is more important than what or how much.

To which customers do you want to give a discount. Again, there should be a clear reason. If you believe that a certain customer is having the potential of giving you more and more business in the near future, then you can give a discount. If you believe that it is a great logo to have in your corporate deck, then you can give a discount. Have a sound logic on whom you are giving the discount. Be aware that giving a discount should not be a default way to win customers.

PRICING – QUESTION-47

How can I make the customers pay for my non-negotiable price?

Great question. That is the state we all want to be in. This is a tough state to achieve. But it is possible. You must be confident to achieve this. More importantly, you should have enough pipeline to achieve this. When you say No, the world respects you. When you stick to your price, there are certain sets of customers who will love that.

With great doctors, lawyers, architects, and auditors you cannot negotiate. They fix their price. It's a non-negotiable price. To achieve that, they have put in a lot of hard work and proved their excellence in their field. Now, they can demand their price and they fix their price. The same with celebrities. They fix their price. You can also do that when you have created a great brand for your product or service. When customers come to you (Inbound leads), then you have a high chance of winning your price.

❖ ❖ ❖

NEGOTIATION – QUESTION-48

There is always a fear that the other party will negotiate better than me. How to overcome that fear?

Fear comes due to a lack of preparation. When you prepare well you will be more confident. In a way, having fear is good; that will make you prepare well and be alert.

The best negotiators are clear about what they want to achieve out of the negotiation. Clarity is important. They are ready to let go of something and very clear about what they will not let go. For example, in a negotiation, you may be willing to compromise on the price to some percentage but very clear that your payment terms will be only 30 days. No extra credit. Having this clarity will help you manage your fear.

NEGOTIATION – QUESTION-49

How should I ensure that I always win in a negotiation?

You should define what you mean by winning. For example, winning means you want to achieve 6 demands in a negotiation and your intention is to achieve all these 6 demands and not agree to any of the other party's demands, then it is not the right objective to achieve.

If winning means having a cordial relationship with the other party even after the negotiation is over, with both parties feeling that they got reasonably what they want, then your objective of always winning in a negotiation makes sense. We should think holistically about how both parties will benefit after the negotiation is over. Both parties need each other for a long-term fruitful relationship.

NEGOTIATION – QUESTION-50

What kind of questions should I ask during a negotiation?

It's good to ask questions to understand what is running in the mind of the other party. Your intention of questioning should be to understand and hear them fully. Actively listen and clearly communicate with your body language that you are listening. Ask more questions to understand better and to have clarity. The best negotiators put themselves in the other person's shoes to understand their point of view.

You should also ask questions to understand what their demands are, which demand is most important to them which they will never compromise, and which demand they may be willing to let go and agree with you. If you can understand this, then it will be easy for you to decide what are the demands you can let go and what are the demands most probably the other party will let go.

NEGOTIATION – QUESTION-51

I want to protect my price during negotiation. How should I do that?

You can protect your price during negotiation. At the same time, you should clearly articulate the value you are giving your customer for the price he/she is paying you. Sometimes you may not be able to convince them of your price, then they may not be your customer. You may have to look out for different target customers who can afford your price.

With some customers, in order to protect the price, you may have to compromise on other terms like payment terms and credit period. Some may not be ready to give you advance if they agree to your price. Great negotiators move the anchor point of discussion from price to some other point.

Say, for example, you can talk about personalization and the prestige the product brings compared to price. I know a textile shop in Bangalore which customizes designer suits for celebrities and that design will not be sold to any other person. Here, the anchor of negotiation is on the design and the buyer is willing to pay the price.

NEGOTIATION – QUESTION-52

When should I walk away from the negotiation?

The most powerful aspect of negotiation is having the courage to walk away from the negotiation. But this should happen rationally, not because of anger, ego, fear, or any other emotion. Before going to the negotiation, you should be clear about your walk-away position. It can be with respect to price, time, volume, quality, or whatever parameter it may be. You should have predicted what may be the range you can negotiate with, on each of these parameters and what is the threshold for each of these parameters above which you cannot operate.

When you have this range clear, then you can negotiate with clarity. If the other party is not ready to do business within this range, then you should politely walk away. Even when walking away from the negotiation, do it gracefully and take care that you save the face for the other party. Meaning, maintaining their respect and dignity.

NEGOTIATION – QUESTION-53

During negotiation I felt that I got a good deal. But when I come out and think about it, I feel I didn't negotiate better. Why is that happening?

It's common for all of us to get that feeling. During negotiation, our mind is in a fear state most of the time. We are worried about the consequence of losing the deal, losing the partnership, losing the relationship based on what we are negotiating. Once the negotiation is done, after one or 2 days, our mind is in a calm state, a rational state. Then when we see the terms, we may feel we could have negotiated better. This happens to most of us. You can avoid this by better preparation. During preparation, write down the objectives you want to achieve out of this negotiation. What are the demands the other party may have, you are ready to agree and ready to disagree. What is the impact of agreeing to those demands and not agreeing to those demands? Gauge the impact for the near term and long-term. Once you put all these on paper and work accordingly, there is a higher probability you will not get that feeling once the negotiation is over.

NEGOTIATION – QUESTION-54

How should I prepare for a negotiation?

One of the good ways to prepare for negotiation is the 4W-1H framework.

W – Who

W – What

W – Where

W – When

H – How

Fill in all these 5 letters. Who are you negotiating with? What is their background? What is their education, experience, preference, etc.? If possible, do complete research on LinkedIn about their past one-year posts. The next one is, what are we negotiating for? What are the aspects we can compromise and what we cannot compromise? Be clear with it.

Next, where is the negotiation happening? Is it in the other party's office, your office, or at a common point? It is better to have the negotiation at a common point. Then, when is the negotiation happening and how long will it happen? Plan for a 50% reduction in time and a 50% extension in time. For different time frames, how will you manage the negotiation? And most importantly, how are you going to do the negotiation, based on facts, stories, examples, emotions, relationships, or a mix of some of these? Have clarity on this. Now do the same 4W, 1H from the shoes of the other party. Prepare for the same. Then you will get a clear idea.

NEGOTIATION – QUESTION-55

What is the one most important aspect I should remember/implement during negotiation?

Instead of one, I will recommend 2 aspects. First, be ready to give something to the other party so that you can get something which you want the most. Second, save the face of the other party. What do I mean by this, save the dignity and respect of the other party. Never bulldoze them.

Even if the negotiation fails, it should happen gracefully. The other party should be ready to work with you in the future. You can disagree on the terms and still respect their views. He/she may forget what you negotiated, what your price was, etc., but they will never forget how you made them feel on that day. Never burn the bridge; you never know what lies ahead in the future.

NEGOTIATION – QUESTION-56

Is it better to avoid negotiation and just accept whatever the customer asks for?

It depends upon the situation you are in. If you are not in a state to negotiate and are desperate to survive, then it is better to accept the terms of the customer but politely ask for help. You may get something out of it.

If you are not in survival mode, then it is always better to negotiate. When you send the proposal, keep in mind that the other party is going to negotiate. When the negotiation happens, what are the things you are ready to let go, add that part of the proposal. During negotiation, you can let go of that and make the other party feel better. Never plan to achieve everything you want. Remember, in negotiation, both parties should win. Only then will the relationship last longer.

SALES CLOSURE – QUESTION-57

How to close every deal I am pursuing?

First, you should understand that you cannot close every deal you are pursuing. This is true for everyone. Irrespective of your capability, and pricing, it is impossible to win all the deals. Because deal closure depends on various parameters. There will be multiple stakeholders in the customer side involved in the decision making. They may have different views based on the context.

For the current context of the customer's company, your solution may not be the right fit. But once they grow further, your solution may be a great fit. Hence, the management would have considered another small vendor. There may be reasons beyond your control on why you are losing. Sometimes it may not be your fault at all. The important thing is to understand why you lose? And be in touch with the customer so that he/she can leverage your solution at the right time. Within your control, do your best and do everything right. This will help you increase the probability of winning.

SALES CLOSURE – QUESTION-58

Until sending the proposal, I am doing things right. But I am not able to close the deals. Why?

There may be multiple reasons for it. Ability to write a great proposal, clearly articulated solution, pricing, handling objections, negotiation, and sales closure – all these skills are needed to close a deal.

You must analyse where there is a need for improvement. Many times, I see entrepreneurs/sales executives struggling to handle objections in a proper way. They talk only from their perspective without understanding the customer's perspective. Sometimes the solution is not articulated clearly in a proposal. It is better to meet/e-meet the client after sending the proposal and explain the proposal in person. Sometimes entrepreneurs/sales executives don't ask closure questions. Without asking closure questions, sales closure will not happen. All the above skills must be consistently developed in order to win more deals.

SALES CLOSURE – QUESTION-59

If I do everything right, will the customer automatically close the deal? Do I have to push for sales closure?

The belief that the customer will automatically close the deal is a very risky proposition. Even if you do everything right, I will still recommend you ask closure questions. Firstly, doing everything right itself is a grey area, as it differs with every customer. Everything right for one customer may be everything minus 2 for another customer. You may have to do 2 more extra things in order to win this client. Every deal is a new learning, and every deal brings new challenges and opportunities. But I can understand when you say doing everything right.

Great salespeople will never take a chance. They will consistently follow up until the deal is closed. They will keep asking closure questions without irritating the customer. They will take care that they are continuously in the mind of the customer. They will connect with all the relevant stakeholders in the customer's organisation. That's how they close the deal consistently.

SALES CLOSURE – QUESTION-60

There is always a fear to ask closure questions. Why is that? How to overcome that?

Fear comes because you are worried about the outcomes. "If I ask a closure question and what if the customer says no," this thought may be running in your mind. Research says 50% of sales executives don't ask closure questions due to fear. You should have the understanding that you cannot win every deal. There is nothing wrong in asking closure questions like "When can we start the project?" "When can I get the purchase order?" "Can we start the installation from tomorrow?" "Are you paying by cash or Cheque?" – all these are closure questions.

When you have enough pipeline, then you will not be afraid to ask closure questions. Imagine, you have sent 10 proposals in the last 2 weeks, then you will not be afraid to ask closure questions. But if you have sent only 2 proposals in the last 3 months, then you are scared. Work hard, build a great pipeline, and ask closure questions without fear.

SALES CLOSURE – QUESTION-61

What are the reasons my deals are not getting closed?

Deals may not get closed for multiple reasons:

1. Customer would have got a better offer on solutions or price from another vendor.
2. Project may be scrapped due to market conditions.
3. Customer is not happy about the way their objections are handled.
4. Customer would have not got a feeling of "Knowledge partner" or "Domain/Functional partner" from your pitch.
5. Customer would have postponed the need for the solution.

Many reasons are possible. For entrepreneurs and sales executives, I always recommend having a strong pipeline. You should forecast/plan for at least a 1:4 ratio for closure: proposal. If you send 4 proposals, one may get closed. In a tough market, make it 1:5.

SALES CLOSURE – QUESTION-62

Customers respond faster until they get a proposal. After getting the proposal, they are silent. They are not communicating with me. How to break this and make them talk to me?

Customers request a proposal because he/she has a problem/need that must be solved. Once you give the proposal, they get an idea of what the proposed solution is and what the corresponding price for it is. Now they can decide when they want to start the project and whom to work with on this project.

It's the responsibility of the entrepreneur/sales executive to continuously follow up with the customer and bring out the explicit and implicit objections. Use your creative mind to follow up in different ways. If needed, go to their office, and wait to meet them. You must follow up and break the silence.

Once you know the objections, handle them effectively and look out for any more objections. If you find more objections, handle them and then ask closure questions which will lead you to closure.

SALES CLOSURE – QUESTION-63

Sometimes customers are so nice to me, and they even give me a hint that this project will be awarded to me. But at the last minute, someone else is winning the deal. Why is that?

This happens to many entrepreneurs/salespeople. There may be 2 important reasons for this. One, the prospective customer may be nice to everybody he/she deals with. It is their default nature. Sometimes, you assume it as a sign that he is going to award the project to you. The second possibility is, that you may be reaching out only to one stakeholder, but the decision would have been made by the consensus of various key stakeholders in the company. The competitor who won the deal would have reached out and been visible to many of the stakeholders, and it would have been a great positive for him/her to win the deal.

It is always prudent to meet various stakeholders/decision-makers during the early stage of the sales cycle. You should ask/influence your champion from the customer organisation to introduce you to various stakeholders.

SALES CLOSURE – QUESTION-64

Is closure the toughest one in the entire sales process?

Sales closure is the most important step in the entire sales process. All other steps are needed only to achieve sales closure. Whether it is the toughest one or not depends on the ability of the entrepreneur/salesperson.

There are many salespeople I know who are good at closing a deal but struggle to generate a lead or are lazy to do a proper follow up. Some of the salespeople are very good at lead generation but struggle a lot to close the deal. They fear asking closure questions. Some of them struggle to negotiate better and because of this, they won't get the approval from the management for the price or payment terms and hence they cannot close the deal.

Hence, closure is a combination of multiple skills. The point to understand is the more skilled person on sales closure should handle closure. If not, you must develop closure skills as it is the most needed skill in sales.

SALES CLOSURE – QUESTION-65

What are some of the metrics I should track in sales closure?

Many metrics lead to sales closure. But the most important metric I prefer is proposal-to-closure ratio. Say for example, last month you have sent 5 proposals and you have closed 3 out of it, then you are very good at negotiation and closure. If, on the other hand, out of the last 10 proposals over the last 3 months you have closed only 2, then you must work on proposal writing, objection handling, negotiation, follow up, and sales closure. Because of the lack of any of these skills or a combination of these skills, maybe the reason for a low closure ratio.

One more metric to track is the negotiation-to-closure ratio. Clients are calling you for negotiation, but you fail to reach an amicable agreement during this meeting. If it happens a lot, then you have to revisit your pricing, objection handling, and negotiation skills to improve your closure.

SALES EXCELLENCE – QUESTION-66

To win a deal, do I have to tell lies?

You don't need to tell lies to win a deal. Telling lies will reduce your probability to win. At the same time, you can show data in a different way. It's all about presenting the data without compromising on the genuity of the data.

Say, for example, you are in a meeting with a prospective customer and the customer is asking, have you done business with automobile companies? The honest answer is no. You can either say no or you can answer like this, "We have worked with many customers in the manufacturing sector who supply components to automobile companies." And it is the truth. It is better than saying "No" as an answer. How you answer a question, and how you position the data is very important in sales.

SALES EXCELLENCE – QUESTION-67

What strengths can introverts leverage to become great salespeople?

It is a wrong notion that extroverts can be greater salespeople than introverts. This is a myth. Each of them has their own strength and they must leverage their strength.

I personally see 2 strengths with introverts which will help them do very well in sales. The first strength is talking less and listening more. Sales is all about asking questions and listening to the answers of the prospect and from that ask more questions. Listening comes naturally to introverts. They must master the art of questioning. Extroverts must work on both listening and questioning. The second strength is, that introverts don't waste their energy by talking too much. They can leverage this energy during sales conversations and cold calls. As we all know, sales is a transfer of energy. If you have energy when you do the pitching, sales happen.

SALES EXCELLENCE – QUESTION-68

How to win the customer in the first meeting?

Yes. You can win the customer in the first meeting by your preparation. When I say winning, it means not getting the purchase order, that may take time. But you can win the mind and heart of the customer by your out-of-the-box preparation.

Preparation itself is a deep subject. When you go beyond normal preparation and ask transformational questions, then the customer will position you as his/her knowledge partner. You will not be seen as any other vendor. You will be seen as a person who is there to solve her problems with your expertise. You can feel it when the customer's body language and tone change and show respect when you ask deep transformational questions.

SALES EXCELLENCE – QUESTION-69

What is the role of discipline in sales success?

Sales is all about discipline. Great salespeople are highly disciplined. Preparation needs discipline. Continuous follow up needs discipline. Response time needs discipline. Proposal writing needs discipline.

Not only in day-to-day activities, but even strategic activities need discipline. Great salespeople have a routine of meeting their top 25 customers every quarter. They keep a record of it and do it consistently. This will also help them to generate new leads from the existing customers. They send minutes of the meeting within 24 hours. Many customers love to work with these salespeople because of their work ethic. Great salespeople keep their word. They do what they say. This needs a disciplined mind. All these disciplined activities result in sales success.

SALES EXCELLENCE – QUESTION-70

What is the one attribute every salesperson should master to become a great salesperson?

According to me, the most important attribute every salesperson should master is the ability to put yourself in the other person's shoes and think. The ability to visualise, you taking the role of the prospective buyer and thinking about what will be their problem? What is the solution they are looking for? What is the price they can afford? What is the risk they are taking? What will be their possible growth concerns? In other words, you should be able to live the life of the prospective person and think from that plane.

When you master this skill, then it will lead you to ask better questions, lead you to understand the prospective buyer better. Understand his/her mind better. At the end of the day, sales is all about understanding the mind of oneself and the mind of the prospective buyer.

SALES EXCELLENCE – QUESTION-71

I am not a natural salesperson. Can I still be successful in sales?

Anybody can be successful in sales provided they are ready to change and learn the concepts of selling. As you said, for some people some of the skills of sales come naturally and for some others, they must put effort to master those skills. The good news is every skill can be learned by practice.

Generally, all human beings are good salespeople when they are born. A child knows how to communicate with her mother when she wants milk. A kid knows how to convince his father to buy a toy for him. As we grow, we develop a fear of rejection and thus start moving away from sales. Sales is easy when you are ready to learn it.

❖ ❖ ❖

SALES EXCELLENCE – QUESTION-72

What are the daily routines of a successful salesperson?

Daily routines vary from person to person. Some of the best salespeople I know follow these routines: They plan their year, quarter, month, week, and day. Every day, at night, they write down their tasks for the next day. If they must meet a client physically, they will map the area and try to cover more prospects/existing clients in that area to build relationships. Every day they do at least 5 follow-ups. They spend at least 15 minutes in the CRM and on LinkedIn. They will have the top 10 possible closures for the month on a sheet of paper and keep it in their purse/bag. They see that sheet every single day and take corresponding actions.

SALES EXCELLENCE – QUESTION-73

Explain the saying "Great salespeople sell less and do more Sales"

It's an amazing phrase. Great salespeople increase the deal size with the right opportunities. Generally, when you get a qualified lead, every salesperson wants to close that deal. Their questioning, their approach will always be to close the deal. But great salespeople control the urge to close; they explore more and see how they can increase the deal size. They do more research, ask transformational questions, gain the respect of the client, and talk about 3-year contracts, and multi-project contracts where the deal size will be 20x, or 30x from the current opportunity. They also know that 9/10 customers may not entertain this and will ask them to focus on the current deal. But that 1/10 customer may say okay for the increased deal size which is 30X. That is equal to winning 30 more clients without any new lead generation or qualification. Thus, they do more sales by doing less selling.

SALES EXCELLENCE – QUESTION-74

How will I know that my sales plan for the year is clear and achievable?

When you first make the plan, you may not be sure whether your plan is clear and achievable. You made that plan based on your forecast of the market, your insights of your existing customers, and your industry experience.

When the year starts and you start talking to the customers in a few weeks, you know whether your plan is going in the right way or not. You should have enough contingency in your plan for market ups and downs. If you are a seasoned entrepreneur or a seasoned salesperson, you may know the pattern of your sales. If you are new to the market, you should better consult with an adviser. No plan is perfect. You should be flexible enough to change the plan every quarter. In some quarters you may have to work hard and take some calculated risks to achieve your target. Sometimes you may have to invest more in your marketing. Be flexible and track your metrics on a weekly basis. Review deeply on a monthly basis and you have a high chance to achieve your plan.

SALES EXCELLENCE – QUESTION-75

I am tired of doing sales every day. I want to stop doing sales and still want to increase my revenue. Is there a way for it?

You cannot increase your revenue without doing sales. It is close to impossible. If you are tired, you can hire a co-founder or a Chief Sales Officer who can do it for you. If you are bored with the current way of doing sales, then you can change your Go-To-Market Strategy. You can think about online sales, distributor sales, or you can think about entering a new country.

This will make your learning very curious, and it will take some time to learn about that country, their culture, etc. That will be exciting for you. You can also introduce a new product or new service and work on finding new customers for this new product. That will keep you busy and interested. All these ideas will also add revenue to your organisation.

SALES PROCESS – QUESTION-76

How should I set sales targets for my organisation?

You can set targets in 2 ways. First, is Inside-out thinking. You see your current year revenue and you know the pulse of the market and you know the bandwidth of your company. Along with all this data, you will also have some hunger for growth. Putting all of this together, you may come up with a growth target of 20%, 50%, or 100% growth.Next way is Outside-in thinking. You don't see inside your organisation. You see the market potential and put a target, saying I should achieve 5% of the market in the next 3 years. Then you work backwards on what should be the target you have to achieve this year which will propel you to achieve 5% in the next 3 years. Nothing is right or wrong. It is based on your hunger for growth.

SALES PROCESS – QUESTION-77

How to review my sales progress?

It's always good to review sales on a weekly, monthly, quarterly, and annual basis. You will have an annual plan and split that into quarterly targets based on your experience of how each quarter differs due to the macro scenario. Say for example, in my business, in the months of December and January, business is less. I must incorporate this into my Oct-Dec and Jan-Mar quarterly targets.

Every week, have clarity on the weekly tasks to be achieved. This must be derived from the monthly sales target, which is set based on the quarterly target. If there is any slowdown in a month, it must be compensated in the following months so that quarterly targets are achieved. If quarterly targets are missed, they must be compensated in the following quarters.

SALES PROCESS – QUESTION-78

What are the key sales metrics I should measure and in what frequency should I measure them?

The key sales metrics you should measure are the leads-to-proposal ratio and proposal-to-closure ratio. If your leads-to-proposal ratio is very low, for example, you have generated 25 leads in the last month and only 2 converted into proposals, then you must improve your ability to present/articulate your company to prospective customers. Also, you should rework your lead generation to target the right customers. If your proposal-to-closure ratio is low, for example, in the last month you sent 10 proposals and only 1 resulted in closure, then you must work on your proposal writing, objection handling, negotiation, and sales closure skills. It is good to check these ratios on a monthly or quarterly basis.

SALES PROCESS – QUESTION-79

How should I plan my sales activities for the week?

Plan your weekly activities based on your monthly target. Create the top 3 goals you want to achieve in a month. For each of these 3 goals, create multiple sub-goals/tasks that must be achieved to reach those 3 monthly goals.

Now allocate those activities for each of the 4 weeks. Plan only for 50% of your week. The remaining 50% of the week is for unexpected problems and new opportunities that were not envisioned. By the start of the month, you must be clear on what you are going to achieve this month, derived from your quarterly goals. Every Sunday night, have a quick run-through of the upcoming weekly tasks.

SALES PROCESS – QUESTION-80

I run a small company. Do I really need a CRM?

Having a CRM (Customer Relationship Management) software is always good. Because today you may be small, but in the next 3 years, you would have interacted with 300-500+ customers. A CRM will have the records of all these customers. It will also help you to analyse the data and make your life easier when you scale. As of now, you can manage with your Excel sheets. But if you can afford a good CRM, I would always recommend that. Today, you get many CRMs at an affordable price. Buying a CRM is not important; you must use it effectively. You should have the discipline to update the data in CRM every single day. Only then can the real benefit of CRM be realised.

SALES PROCESS – QUESTION-81

What are the important tools I need to have to run my sales organisation effectively?

My personal recommendation is that you should subscribe to the Microsoft Office package. Have a good email provider like Gmail, Outlook, or Zoho. You should also have an enterprise account of Zoom, Google Meet, or Microsoft Teams. You should have a premium LinkedIn subscription. You can also use easyleadz, apollo.io, Adapt.io, or Lusha for lead generation. With respect to CRM, you can choose Zoho, HubSpot, or Teleduce. Use Canva to create your flyers. You can use the trial version of the above software and based on your user experience, you can purchase them. All these software/subscriptions are important for a sales organisation. I know a few companies that buy the subscription but never use it. It's important to use them regularly to get the desired results.

SALES STRATEGY – QUESTION-82

Who is my customer?

This is the most important question every entrepreneur/sales executive should ask themselves. Because every 2-3 years, the answer to this question will change. Based on how the world is changing, the market is changing, you are changing, your product is changing, your past few-year-old customers may not be your customers today.

The clarity to understand who my customer is will propel the growth of your company. Sometimes, a customer may leave you, as you are not their supplier for the current context, and sometimes you will drop your customer because they are not your customer for your current context.

For example, 12-15 years back, Indian automobile companies were selling entry-level cars, hatchbacks as their highest-selling models. But now in the year 2024, SUVs are the fastest-growing segment. As a company, if you don't change as per the market scenario, then you are out of the market.

SALES STRATEGY – QUESTION-83

How to get the first 10 customers?

When you launch a product or service, nobody believes in you because nobody knows the quality of your product or service. But there are people who know you as a person. You have built credibility as a human being. Reach out to your friends, family members, college classmates, school classmates, apartment complex friends who have interacted with you. Ask them for connections in the corporate world. Leverage their credibility and go and meet with prospective customers.

Give your product/service free for the first few months and in return ask for feedback and a written testimonial. Once 8-10 companies are using your product/service whether paid or not, you will get confidence. With this feedback, confidence you can go to the market and win paying customers. In short, your first 10 customers will come from your known contacts.

SALES STRATEGY – QUESTION-84

What should be my priority? Whether to get more new clients or whether to get more revenue from my existing clients year on year?

I would recommend doing both. Getting more new clients is important as it is impossible to retain 100% of clients all the time. For various reasons, which are not in your control, you may lose an existing client. Hence, you should always work on getting new clients. Your learning will also be new. You can also get better pricing.

At the same time, you should also work on getting more revenue from existing clients. It is comparatively easy. You know their business now; you already have a good relationship. You also know the gap in their business. You can help them grow by filling that gap and adding value to them. It's a win-win situation.

SALES STRATEGY – QUESTION-85

I am not able to retain more than 50% of my customers. What should I do?

You can lose some percentage of clients but 50% is too big. It may happen due to various reasons. One of the reasons may be you are not able to add more value to their business. They have considered you as a stop-gap arrangement. Another reason may be you are not farming well.

Have account managers for each account and the role of the account managers is to delight the customer, be a single point of contact for them and work on increasing more revenue from that customer. He/she should not only retain the customer but also should get more revenue from the customer. If you are the CEO of the company, then you should visit your top 25 customers periodically. At least once in a quarter you should meet them or should have a call with them.

SALES STRATEGY – QUESTION-86

When will I know I must win bigger clients and bigger deals?

You are already ready for it. You must believe it. That's all. It's all in the mind. If you believe you need another 5 years to reach there, then it will happen in 5 years. If you believe it will happen by next year, then it will happen by next year.

When your mind believes it, it will search for relevant data in the world to prove it. You will start generating leads only with big clients for bigger orders. You may initially fail in a few proposals but after that, you will start winning big deals. You will start going to conferences and seminars where big clients are participating. Your entire action changes once belief changes.

❖ ❖ ❖

SALES STRATEGY – QUESTION-87

How to sell when a customer's business is not doing well?

You can see this in 2 ways. First, you can be loyal to your customer. Support them when they need help. Don't sell anything new but support them for their growth. Help them with payment terms, credit periods if you can afford to do that. Recommend their business to your contacts if possible.

Second, this is also a good alert for you to have customers in multiple industries. Ideally, only 25% of your business should come from one industry. For example, if travel and tourism are down and you have another 75% of business coming from other verticals, then you got hit only by 25% of business which is from travel and tourism. This de-risking is very important. To summarise, help your customer wherever possible when their business is not doing well. Make your business in some other verticals with other customers.

SALES STRATEGY – QUESTION-88

I am building a great product. I believe sales will happen automatically. Do I still have to sell?

Even if you have a great product, you must still sell. The world doesn't know that you have a great product. Also, when the prospective buyer is intending to buy, they should have a great buying experience. Else, he/she may not buy.

Apple creates some of the great products in the world. Still, Apple has hundreds of sales employees across the world to sell the products. Not only that, sales executives can also cross-sell and up-sell. If you go to an Apple shop to buy a MacBook Air, you may end up buying a MacBook Air, an iPad, and an iPhone. That's why you need a sales team. Also, you may even buy 3 iPhones for your entire family instead of one if the salesperson convinces you with the right relevant questions.

SALES STRATEGY – QUESTION-89

How to win over competition?

The best way to win the competition is to ignore it. Whatever you focus on expands. If you think more about your competition, fear expands. By focusing on the competition, you are also limiting your growth by comparing it with the growth of the competition.

To achieve limitless growth, there is only one competition. That is your own data for the last year. You compete with yourself. Every year, you beat your own sales, your own records. Focus on excellence. Continuously improve your product/service. Learn continuously, attend conferences across the world. Learn from everybody. Innovate consistently. Competition is irrelevant.

SALES STRATEGY – QUESTION-90

As an entrepreneur, how much time should I allocate to sales?

The better question will be, as an entrepreneur, how much time should I allocate to non-sales activities? Because sales is your primary activity. You should delegate most of your work. You should spend more time with your customers, understanding their problems. You should be in the field talking, observing your customers.

If you are not good at sales, hire a sales co-founder or hire a Chief Sales Officer, or learn sales. You should do either of the 3. I will still prefer you learning sales. Every entrepreneur should learn sales whether he/she likes it or not.

SALES STRATEGY – QUESTION-91

When I am trying to sell my product, the prospective customer is asking for a new feature. When I built that feature, they are not buying it. What should I do?

It typically happens to all new product startups. Remember every new feature you are adding is a cost to the company. There is no end to adding new features. We must balance between listening to the market and the cost involved in it. I recommend once you are ready with basic features which are solving the key problems of the customers, go to the market and start selling. You can always add more features in the upcoming release. Don't keep updating new features just because one prospective customer asks for it.

You should start making money from the product. Paying customers are a great source of honest feedback. If a paying customer is asking for a new feature and when you say you will add extra cost for it and if they agree to it, then it is worth building that feature immediately.

SALES STRATEGY – QUESTION-92

How should I balance growth and the cost involved for growth?

As you rightly asked, growth comes with a cost. Too much growth in a single quarter or year may also break you. Have a forecast on sales and cost. If you grew 20% quarter on quarter what will be the impact on delivery? People? Infrastructure? Cash flow? etc. How to manage the funds for it? Are you going to raise debt with banks or raise money with equity? All these questions are important.

If the growth exceeds 20% and say you are growing at 50% in the next quarter and you are not able to manage the delivery due to cash flow issues, then you are spoiling your brand in the market. Cash flow management is as important as sales. Good sales and bad delivery are a recipe for disaster. Repeat sales happen only because of great delivery. Balanced growth is the way forward. If you are growing super-fast, plan your finance and delivery well in advance.

SALES STRATEGY – QUESTION-93

How should I create a sales strategy and when should I create it?

If you follow the January to December financial year, you should start your sales planning by August of the previous year. In many ways, you can create your sales strategy. Let me share a simple way: NP-NC, NP-OC, OP-NC, OP-OC.

1. New Product – New Customer
2. New Product – Old Customer
3. Old Product – New Customer
4. Old Product – Old Customer

You can replace 'product' with 'service' as well. Forecast your sales by allocating percentage revenue for each of these categories. Generally, OP-OC should have more revenue forecast, say 50%, and OP-NC may have a 20% revenue forecast. NP-OC may have another 15-20%, and NP-NC may have 10-15%. The percentage will vary based on your product and industry.

If you are convinced of the above strategy or similar such numbers, then work accordingly by meeting your existing old clients and generating leads for new clients. It is comparatively easy to sell to your old clients. You get repeat business from them.

SALES STRATEGY – QUESTION-94

Every year how many new customers should I win?

This depends on your growth hunger. This also depends on how much percentage of business will come from your existing customers. But it is always good to build a pipeline and talk to new customers.

If you are happy with the number of customers you have currently and your bandwidth is almost full and you are getting new customers, then it is the best time to increase your price. With the new customers, increase your price; even if you lose, there is no impact for you. It is the best state to be in, which is very rare. In this way, you may not win more customers, but every new addition of customers will bring more value/revenue for you.

SALES STRATEGY – QUESTION-95

When will I know I should enter new markets/new countries for expansion?

You must consider a few aspects before you enter a new market/country. The first question is why do you want to enter a new country? Is your product/service ready for that new country? Will you be able to invest for the first one-year to understand and accommodate that market? Other than revenue, what is the strategic value the new market is bringing to your company? What is your Go-To-Market Strategy for that country? Are you going to have your own sales team? Or are you going to have distributors in that country? Or are you going to sell online in that country? All these questions must be answered.

It is better to talk to an adviser like me or a similar sales coach and take inputs or hire their service before entering a new country. It will take a lot of your time and effort. It is wiser to prepare well before taking that decision.

SALES STRATEGY – QUESTION-96

How to decide whether I should add new products or services or continue with my existing product or service?

This again depends on your growth hunger and market need. Great companies disrupt themselves with new products and services. They will also spend a lot of effort to upgrade their current product and service to suit the current market needs.

For the last 20+ years, I am using Microsoft Office products. Still, I like it. It has changed a lot. Even with so many competitors, still, I like Microsoft Word, Excel, and PowerPoint. At the same time, Microsoft has launched so many new products. We must learn from these corporates.

Don't kill your cash cow. Improve your current product and service. At the same time, innovate and invest in new products and services.

❖ ❖ ❖

SALES TEAM – QUESTION-97

When should I hire a sales team?

If you are a startup founder or a new business owner, then I recommend for the first 2 years, you should do the sales. By doing the sales, you will understand the customers better. You will understand what is needed in the market.

Once you have sold to 100 customers or crossed 2 years in selling, then start building a sales team. Now you will have the ability to ask the right questions to your team. If your team is asking you a question, then you will be able to give a right answer to them.

If you are an established business owner for 3+ years and you have done sales all through your entrepreneurial life, then you should hire a sales team to grow further.

SALES TEAM – QUESTION-98

What if the salesperson doesn't deliver as per my expectation?

First, you have to clearly communicate your expectations to the salesperson when you hire them. This communication should be both verbal and, in a document/mail. You should also have a plan on how you will support that person to achieve their target. Generally, I ask all my sales team to give me a '100-day plan' when they are hired. What is it that they want to achieve in the first 100 days in the company? We will have this discussion in the first week of their joining the company.

I also recommend you set a meeting in the calendar to review with the new hire for the first 30, 60, and 90th day. Send this calendar invite to them in the first week. During this review, you should evaluate their performance and give feedback. You should fire them within these 90 days if you are not satisfied. If you are happy in the first 90 days, then you should have patience until the end of the first year for their performance review.

SALES TEAM – QUESTION-99

How to measure the performance of my sales team?

The best way to measure the performance of the sales team is by the revenue they bring in. For the existing sales team, it's purely numbers. Also, compare their revenue numbers with previous years. There should be a growth trend. You should also insist on getting new customers.

Many times, sales executives will be comfortable achieving their numbers by the repeat orders of existing customers and by increasing the revenue from existing customers. Though this is very important, this alone will not suffice. Every sales executive should also win new clients. Preferably win new clients with a better price. Also, you should work with them to focus on bigger deals which will bring predictability in revenue.

SALES TEAM – QUESTION-100

I am not able to trust my sales team. What if they take my customer when they leave the company?

It's a very tricky question. This has happened to some of my customers. In that company, most of the customer relationships were handled by a senior person and when he left the company after working for 10 years, the client lost more than 50% of the revenue.

If you are the founder of the company, you should build a good rapport with your top 25 customers. If you are a small to medium-sized company, your top 25 customers generally account for 80% of business. If you are a large company, you should have a good rapport with your top 100 customers. Also, every customer detail has to be captured in CRM diligently. This should be a company culture. Any review should happen only from the data of the CRM. This way you can mitigate the risk to some extent.

SALES TEAM – QUESTION-101

How to create a proper incentive structure for my sales team?

Incentives are most important for a sales team. Generally, I recommend a 3-point plan for the sales team. Every sales member should get a fixed salary, variable salary, and sales commission (bonus). Variable pay depends on the performance of the company or business unit and the performance of the individual. Sales commission can be a percentage of Gross Profit or Revenue based on the company policy.

I personally recommend gross profit. If you are not able to calculate gross profit, assume it as 40%. From that number, you can give 5% as sales commission. For example, if the deal closed is USD 100K then gross profit is 40K and 5% of 40K is USD 2000. That will be the sales commission which roughly comes to 2% of the revenue. For repeat business, you can give 50% of this 2 % which is 1% of the total revenue.

SALES TEAM – QUESTION-102

When and how should I fire my non-performing salesperson?

First, you should strengthen your hiring process. During hiring itself, you should be able to analyse and reasonably judge whether he/she will suit your company culture.Sales are driven by numbers. It is easy to gauge the performance of a salesperson compared to other department executives. If a salesperson is not performing for 2 consecutive quarters, then you should warn him/her that they will have only one more quarter to prove their performance. If the 3rd quarter is also below the par performance, then you can make your decision regarding firing. Your monthly review itself will catch the performance lag. Three months is a good time period for any salesperson to improve their performance.

SALES TEAM – QUESTION-103

Do I need to have a daily review with my sales team?

You don't need to have a daily review with your sales team, but you can have a quick stand-up meeting with them. In today's world, anybody can join the call from anywhere. Every morning at 9 am, having a quick 15-minute call with your sales team will bring discipline. When I had my sales team, I used to have daily calls. Everyone would quickly update what their plan for the day was and what the outcome of yesterday was.

Any detailed discussion can happen on a scheduled call. This morning call should not go beyond 10-15 minutes. It creates a bond between the leader and the sales team. I strongly recommend daily stand-up meetings.

SALES TEAM – QUESTION-104

What are the key attributes I should look for when I am hiring a new sales executive?

Attitude is the most important attribute you should look for in a sales executive. You can create specific case scenarios and ask them to write or explain how they interpreted and how they will react to that scenario. I would prefer them to write it on a sheet and then explain it to me in a face-to-face meeting. I prefer a case study-based interview process.

I would also check the ability to ask deep, meaningful questions in a sales executive. The ability to listen is super important. Their way of dressing, their communication, all these are important.

SALES TEAM – QUESTION-105

Is it better to have your own sales team or to have distribution partners? Which is the best way to do sales?

It depends on your product and industry. If it is customary in your industry to do business through distributors, then follow the same. If that is not the case, and if you can afford to have your own sales team, then go ahead with that approach. Having your own sales team on the ground has many benefits. You have control over your growth. You get many data points. Your relationship with the customer will be very strong. It also depends on whether you are doing B2B business (Business to Business) or B2C business (Business to Consumer).

B2B businesses generally have their own sales team, and B2C businesses prefer distributorship/dealership.

SALES TEAM – QUESTION-106

I am not able to hire good salespeople. Even if I hire them, good salespeople are not staying for a long time. How to solve this?

Hiring good salespeople is tough. In the market, the supply of good salespeople is less compared to the demand. Hence it is very important to retain good salespeople.

Good salespeople are optimistic, have high energy, and look for freedom. If you want to retain them, give them freedom. Listen to them often and allow them to express their ideas. Give them tough targets and support them to achieve it. When they achieve it, reward them generously and recognise them for their talent. Most of the top talent stays in the company based on how they are treated by their boss. If you are an amazing leader, then the probability of retaining your top salespeople is high.

SALES TEAM – QUESTION-107

What is the right structure for a sales team? I prefer to hire one senior salesperson and delegate all my sales responsibility. Is that a good strategy?

It depends on your company size, your selling ability, and your hunger for growth. If you are a startup, for the first 2 years, I recommend you, as the founder, to do sales. If you are a company that has been in the business for 5-7+ years, then you need to have a structured sales team.Hire a good senior salesperson or promote somebody who is with you for a long-term and who has the leadership capability. Give him/her the freedom to create his/her team. Even after all this, you cannot completely delegate the sales responsibility. You must meet your top 25 customers. You must know the pulse of the market as a founder. You should have sales review with your sales head every week.

❖ ❖ ❖

SALES TEAM – QUESTION-108

Will a remote sales teamwork? I prefer to hire salespeople across the country. I cannot have offices across the country. Will this work?

I know many companies that are working with this model. You must build trust within your team. It's preferable to choose somebody who has worked with you for a few years, promote them, and send them to a new city as a city head.

He/She can create a team under them. Wherever the team is, I recommend you should have a quarterly face-to-face meeting and an annual conference where all your sales executives are together for at least 2-3 days. This bonding and cross-knowledge will help. Daily stand-up meetings and weekly reviews will ensure that no red flags are missed. To summarise, this remote model may work provided there is the right process and deep trust within the team.

Recommended Books for further reading

I recommend my readers to buy and read the following books to enhance their sales knowledge. I respect and appreciate all the below authors for contributing their knowledge to the world

- Positioning: The battle of your mind by Al Ries & Jack Trout
- The 22 Immutable laws of Marketing by Al Ries & Jack Trout
- Be a Sales Super Star by Brian Tracy
- You can Sell: Results are rewarded, efforts aren't by Shiv Khera
- Secrets of Closing the Sale by Zig Ziglar
- Anybody can Sell by Subramanian Chandramouli
- Sales for Startups by Subramanian Chandramouli
- Don't spend money for generating leads by Subramanian Chandramouli
- The Ultimate Sales Machine by Chet Holmes

About the Author

Subramanian Chandramouli is the founder of Vrddhi Business Solutions. He conducts sales training and sales mentoring across many countries. He has trained more than 13,000 people in various aspects of sales. He has trained 46 different nationalities that include people from Asia, Europe, North America and Africa. He does a lot of programmes in the Middle East.

- Some of his training programmes are:
- Be a Sales Super Star
- Inside Sales
- Advanced Selling Skills
- Account Management (Sales for Delivery team)
- Customer Delight
- Negotiation skills
- Pricing for Profit
- Business Story Telling
- Entrepreneurial Mindset
- Sales for Startups
- Decision Making
- Negotiation skills for Procurement Team
- Advanced Negotiation Skills
- Conflict Management
- Influencing Skills
- Building Trust
- Personal Effectiveness
- Leadership through Movies
- Presentation skills

- ✓ He is a speaker at SAARC, IIM – Kozhikode, SP Jain School of Global Management.
- ✓ He is a certified **MahaAcharya** Trainer. "Train the Trainer" programme by **Prof. Srinivasan Ranganathan and Meena.**
- ✓ Certified "Train the Trainer" of **T. Harv Eker's** signature TTT Programme.
- ✓ Certified in "**SPIN Selling**" by Huthwaite Singapore.
- ✓ He is also a visiting professor for sales at SP Jain School of Global Management – Dubai & Mumbai and Mahindra University – Hyderabad.

If you want to get trained by Subramanian, or to have paid one to one consulting/mentoring sessions or for speaking assignment, you can reach out to him at subramanian@subbu.co

You can visit his website www.subbu.co for more details. You can follow him on Facebook at @subbusalestrainer and in LinkedIn at https://in.linkedin.com/in/subramaniancm

Annual Sales Excellence Programme

231

Subramanian Chandramouli has a mission to transform 1 million entrepreneurs and sales executives. One of the ways he wanted to help entrepreneurs and sales executives is through his Annual Sales Excellence Programme.

This programme generally starts in January and July of every year and runs for 12 months. The complete programme is done online. It's a live training programme where participants will have a 3-hour session every month. They will also be part of a WhatsApp group where their doubts are clarified. For one-year, they are given hand holding on their sales challenges. Total 36 hours of live training sessions. Participants from India, Dubai, Saudi Arabia, and Sri Lanka are part of current batch. If you want to join either January or July batch you can write a mail to subramanian@subbu.co and block your seat.

SUBRAMANIAN CHANDRAMOULI
ANYBODY
CAN SELL
Practical Tips to Master the Art of Selling

SUBRAMANIAN CHANDRAMOULI

SALES FO₹ STARTUP$

STEP BY STEP GUIDE TO CREATE EFFECTIVE
SALES STRATEGY AND PROCESSES FOR STARTUPS

SUBRAMANIAN CHANDRAMOULI
DON'T SPEND MONEY FOR GENERATING LEADS
A Sales Classic on Lead Generation

www.ingramcontent.com/pod-product-compliance
Lightning Source LLC
Chambersburg PA
CBHW031538150726
47990CB00001B/222